AESCHYLUS

The Libation Bearers
and
The Eumenides

Crofts Classics

GENERAL EDITORS

R. C. Bald, *University of Chicago*
Samuel H. Beer, *Harvard University*
William C. DeVane, *Yale University*

AESCHYLUS

The Libation

Bearers

and

The Eumenides

THE ORESTEIA:

PARTS II AND III

TRANSLATED AND EDITED BY

Peter D. Arnott

STATE UNIVERSITY OF IOWA

APPLETON-CENTURY-CROFTS

Educational Division

New York MEREDITH CORPORATION

introduction

The Libation Bearers and The Eumenides are the second and third parts of the Oresteia (Saga of Orestes) dealing with the misfortunes of the family of Atreus, the royal house of Argos. Atreus quarreled with his brother Thyestes, and to punish him killed his children and served their bodies to him as part of a feast. In retaliation Thyestes laid a curse on Atreus' descendants. The first play of the trilogy, Agamemnon, is set in Argos immediately after the Trojan War, and shows the working of the curse on the next generation. Agamemnon, Atreus' elder son, had been exposed by the circumstances of the war to both public and private resentment. He had alienated his people by entering a war which they felt was none of their concern. He had been forced, even before the Greek fleet sailed to Troy, to sacrifice his daughter Iphigeneia to appease the divine wrath, thereby forfeiting the affection of his wife Clytemnestra. Further, he had offended the gods themselves by his wanton destruction of their temples when Troy eventually fell. On his return to Argos he is murdered by Clytemnestra and her lover Aegisthus, Thyestes' only surviving son. This is the first stage of the Curse. Orestes, son of Agamemnon and Clytemnestra, had been sent out of Argos by his mother during the war, while he was still a small child. Agamemnon ends with Clytemnestra and Aegisthus imposing their tyranny on the city, while the chorus, representing the elders of Argos, look forward to Orestes' return as their only hope of revenge and salvation. When The Libation Bearers opens, Orestes, now grown to manhood, has returned secretly to Argos to plot the punishment of his father's murderers.

principal dates in the life
of Aeschylus

B.C.	525/4	Aeschylus born at Eleusis, near Athens
	490	Fights with Athenian army against Persians at Marathon
	484	First victory in dramatic festival at Athens
	480	Fights in battle of Salamis
	472	Production of *The Persians*
	468	Defeated in dramatic festival by Sophocles
	467	Production of *Seven Against Thebes*
	c. 465	Production of *The Suppliant Women*
	?	First visit to Sicily to supervise productions of his plays; returns to Athens
	458	Production of the *Oresteia* trilogy
	?	Production of *Prometheus Bound*
	?	Second visit to Sicily
	456	Dies at Gela in Sicily

NOTE: The information on Aeschylus' life is scanty, and often rests on inferences from unreliable sources. He is said to have written over eighty plays; the above table notes only those that we still possess. Of these, the dates of *The Suppliant Women* and *Prometheus Bound* are still doubtful. *The Suppliant Women* was long thought to be the earliest play of Aeschylus, and thus the earliest Greek tragedy, that we possessed, but most scholars now agree in placing it considerably later. *Prometheus Bound*, which was also long thought to be an early play, is now commonly believed to have been written towards the end of Aeschylus' life. Some scholars would go so far as to believe that it should not be attributed to Aeschylus at all, but to a later imitator of his style.

the libation bearers

dramatis personae

ORESTES, son of the late king AGAMEMNON and CLYTEM-
NESTRA
ELECTRA, his sister
CLYTEMNESTRA, Queen of Argos
AEGISTHUS, CLYTEMNESTRA's lover, now King of Argos
CILISSA, ORESTES' old nurse
PYLADES, friend of ORESTES
PORTER,
SERVANT, of AEGISTHUS
CHORUS, of slavewomen

SCENE: at first, by the grave of AGAMEMNON; later,
before the door of the royal palace.

THE LIBATION BEARERS

[*The grave of* AGAMEMNON. ORESTES *kneels in prayer.*
His friend PYLADES *stands silent at a distance*]

ORESTES. Hermes, spirit of the underworld
And father's regent, lend to me
Your strength, and stand my champion, I pray,
For I have come home to my land again
And on this mounded tomb invoke my father
To listen and attend.

[*Laying a lock of hair upon the grave*]

A lock of hair to Inachus, for manhood;
Its fellow here, as token for the dead;
For I was not at hand to mourn your passing,
My father, or salute your burial.   10

[*The* CHORUS *of mourning women, with* ELECTRA
among them, appear in the distance. They carry urns
with libations to pour over the grave]

But what is here now? What processional

---

1 **Hermes** messenger-god, one of whose functions was to escort
the spirits of the dead to the underworld. Thus he is frequently
appealed to, both in this play and *The Eumenides* as the in-
termediary between the living and the dead.
7 **a lock of hair** common votive offering, particularly in acts of
mourning. **Inachus** river-god of Argos

3

Of women, in dignity of mourning black,
Is coming? What should I make this to mean?
A signal of new sorrow for the palace?
Or am I to suppose these women bring
Libations as late offerings to my father?
So it must be; for I think I see my sister
Electra among them, grief scored bold
Upon her face. Zeus, give me revenge
20 For my dead father; be my willing aid.
Pylades, let us give them room.
I must assure myself about this cry of women.

[ORESTES *and* PYLADES *conceal themselves as the
women approach the grave*]

CHORUS. Forth from the palace gates, as I was bid,
With urns I come, with drumming hands,
Torn cheeks, the nails' fresh furrows
A talisman of red,
And in my heart old sorrow;
With rending of my robes, with fingers tearing
Wild at the linen on my breast
30 In grief of glad days gone.

For in the dead watch Fright with streaming hair
Shrilled from its cell, and to the dreaming house
Told things to come, a gust of rancor stirring
Fresh out of slumber,
Beating ironfisted on the doors
Of women. The seers swore by the gods their masters

31 **Fright with streaming hair** personification of Clytemnestra's
prophetic nightmare, recounted more explicitly in vv. 555ff.
Shrilled from its cell the language deliberately suggests the ap-
paratus of Apollo's oracular shrine at Delphi

That anger was pulsing in the grave
Against the murderers.

So in hollow office of appeasement,
Earth, O Earth, in mock of holy law,   40
She sends me forth. But there is fear
At such a word.
For who can ransom blood once spilled
On the ground? O joyless hearth,
O desolation of our house,
Sun hid his face, the pestilence
Of darkness fell thick on our palace
At the killing of our kings.

The splendor of our yesterdays, that stood
Triumphant, matchless and invincible   50
To thrill men's hearts with story, is departed
And terror comes.
Success is god, and greater than god
For mortal men. But Justice holds
Her balance attentive, coming swift
On some by day, for some waits ripening
Till evenfall, and those remaining
Are swallowed up in night.

Blood poured for mother earth to drink
Lies crusted, a living sore   60
To cry revenge. Destruction works
On the sinner, spiking him with plague
Till he is rotten through.

As once the chambers of virginity
Are forced, there is no remedy,

So all the waters of the world
Would seek to wash blood clean from guilty
Hands, and do their work in vain.

On me and on mine the gods imposed
70 The hard necessity of conquest
And from the dwellings of my fathers
Brought me here to be a slave.
So I can do no other but approve
My masters, right or wrong—my life
Is new come in their keeping,
And I must struggle to suppress
The heart's loathing.
But still there run behind the veil
Tears for the errant destiny of kings
80 And to the secret places of my heart
Comes the cold touch of horror.

[ELECTRA *takes her place at the graveside*]

ELECTRA. You serving-maids, who set our house to
rights,
Since you have trod this path of prayer with me,
Give me your counsel here. How should I speak
As I pour these offerings on my father's grave?
With what address, what sacramental words?
That this is love's commission to her love,
To husband from his wife—and this my mother?
I would not dare. Then what accompaniment
90 Should herald these libations underground?
I know not. Or could I say this—
That men believe that those who send such wreaths
As these, deserve to be repaid in kind
With presents worthy of their merits?
Or should I pour into the thirsty earth
Without a word, without a salutation,

In manner as he died, and fling the urn away
As one who would be rid of it forever,
And go my way without a backward glance?
This is the question, friends. Advise me.   100
We share a roof, a common hate.
So do not hide your counsels out of fear
Of . . . anyone. The free man and the slave,
Each has his destiny. So speak;
Perhaps you know a better.

   CHORUS. If you will have it so, I'll speak my mind
Before your father's tomb, which is for me
A sacred shrine—
   EL.   Then as you reverence
My father's grave, speak to me now.
   CHORUS. Pour, and call blessings on men of good-
      will—   110
   EL. And where among my friends could I find any
To bear that name?
   CHORUS. Yourself; then anyone who hates Aegisthus.
   EL. You, then, and me. Is that to be my prayer?
   CHORUS. You know what I mean. But you must say
it.
   EL. Whom else shall I number in this company?
   CHORUS. Remember Orestes, banished though he be.
   EL. That was well spoken, my good instructor.
   CHORUS. And for the ones who shed this blood, re-
      member—
   EL. What? I am strange to this, you must dictate to
      me.   120
   CHORUS. To call someone against them, from this
      world
Or from the other—
   EL. To judge, or to revenge? Explain yourself.
   CHORUS. In plain words, to take life for life.

EL. May I so pray, without offence to heaven?
CHORUS. Why not? To pay your enemy in kind?
   EL. God of darkness, Hermes, potent messenger
Of this world and the next, I summon you
To help me now, and call
130 The spirits of the underworld, that watch
My father's house, to hear me as I pray,
And summon Earth, that brings all things to life
And takes her rearing to her womb again.
As I pour out these vessels to the dead,
I call upon my father. Pity me,
And light Orestes' lamp within our house,
For we are homeless now, our mother's chattels
With which she purchased for herself a man,
Aegisthus, who was partner in your murder.
140 I am no better than a slave; Orestes
Is banished from his rich inheritance,
While they loll back in luxury, and reap
The harvest of your labor. Thus I pray,
My father, listen close. Let fortune bring
Orestes home, and let me show myself
More modest than my mother was, my hand
More virtuous.
   These prayers for us. This for our enemies:
Father, I charge you show us your avenger.
150 Kill them who killed you. Render them this justice.
And let me set against their curse
My curse, to fall on them.
Bring us blessings from the underworld;
The gods be on our side, and Earth,
And justice triumphant.
Such is the litany to which I pour
These offerings.
   [*To the* CHORUS] And you, as the custom is,

Must crown the prayers with your lament, and sing
Your hymnal to the dead.

    CHORUS. Let fall now for the fallen lord   160
A watering of tears
As pitchers are upturned
On this holy mound, a bastion
Against evil, and a curse that must be laid.
Hear me, majesty; lord, as you lie dim,
Give this your mind. What champion will rise
To be our palace's deliverance?
What warrior to wield the backbent
Bow of Scythia, or come
Firmhilted to the handfight?   170

    EL. The earth has drunk. My father has his due.

[Seeing the lock of ORESTES' *hair]*

But here is something strange to tell,
Something for all of us.

    CHORUS. Tell me what you mean.
Fear is stepping nimble in my heart.

    EL. Look, on the tomb. A lock of hair.

    CHORUS. Whose? Man's or woman's?

    EL. Guess. Nobody could mistake it.

    CHORUS. What is it? Your young years must teach
    my age.

    EL. This curl could not have come from any head 180
But mine.

    CHORUS. His nearest hate him, they would never
Cut hair in his mourning.

    EL. But look at it—so very like—

    CHORUS. Like whose hair? Tell me.

    EL. My own. So like. Compare them.

169 **Bow of Scythia** the Scythians were famous archers in an-
tiquity

CHORUS. Orestes? Has he come in secret
To make this offering?
    EL.   Yes, he has hair
Like this.
    CHORUS. He would not dare to come.
190 EL. He sent it, then; this shorn lock,
A lovegift to his father.
    CHORUS. Then I have no less cause to weep
If he will never set foot in this land again.
    EL. I too. The full tide of my anger now
Has come, it is a knife to rend my heart.
The dyke is down, the tears fall from my eyes
Unslaked, my grief is at the flood
To see this hair. Oh, how could I imagine
That this lock could have come from any other
200 In Argos? It was not the murderess
That cropped her hair, my mother—what a name
For her, that fiend who hates her children!
But how can I say straight and clear
This glory comes from him I love the best,
Orestes—oh, I am hope's fool!
If it had wit to speak, if it could tell me,
Then I should not be torn between two minds,
But know for sure if I should cast it out
For being fathered by a head I hate
210 Or if it is one blood with mine, my sorrow's partner
To grace this grave, and reverence my father.
But on the gods we call, who know
What tempests have beset our voyaging,
And if it is ordained we come safe home,
Great trunks from little seeds may grow.

        [*Seeing footprints on the ground*]

A second witness! Marks upon the ground

Like those my feet have made, the very same . . .
No, there's a double set of footprints here,
One his, and one somebody's that was with him. . . .
The heel, the tracing of the toes; these measurements 220
Exactly fit with mine—I cannot bear it!
This is too much to think of!

[ORESTES *and* PYLADES *step from their hiding place*]

OR. You may inform the gods your prayers are an-
    swered.
Now pray to be as lucky in the future.
    EL. Why? What favor have I won from them?
    OR. You are in sight of what you prayed to see so
    long.
    EL. The man I prayed for—what is he to you?
    OR. I know how you long to see Orestes.
    EL. What makes you think my prayers are answered?
    OR. Here I am. Look no further. You will never find 230
A closer friend.
    EL. I do not know you. Are you playing tricks on
    me?
    OR. If so, I play a trick upon myself.
    EL. Have you come here to laugh at my misfortunes?
    OR. If they are your misfortunes, they are mine.
    EL. Let me pretend you are Orestes, then,
And bid you—
    OR.   I am Orestes,
And you do not know me when you see me.
But when you saw this hair cut off in mourning,
When you looked on the earth my feet had trod,   240
Your mind flew on the instant to the thought
That what you saw was me.
Look, lay this lock of hair where it was cut;
It is your brother's—see, it matches yours.

[*Showing a child's garment*]

And look, the jerkin that you wove for me:
The texture, this embroidery of beasts—

[ELECTRA *is convinced, and weeps for joy*]

Control yourself, and do not let your joy
Outweigh discretion. I am well acquainted
With our dear friends, and how they hate us.

250   EL. Oh dearest treasure of our father's house,
Its hope, its future seed; how we have wept for you.
It shall be yours again. You have your father's strength
Behind you. Face that I have longed to see;
You have divided me, and made four loves from one.
One for my father—that is your name now;
One for my loving duty to my mother—
Her share is yours; to her I give my hate;
One for my sister's cruel sacrifice;
One for the brother true that I have found you,
260 The only one of all my family
To give me dignity.
So Might and Justice fight upon my side
And Zeus Almighty, greatest of them all,
To make a third.
      OR. Zeus, O Zeus, look down at what has passed here.
Look at us both, the eagle's children,
Parentless, their father strangled
In the deadly embraces of a snake.
Their father's dead, and they must starve,
270 For they have not his art, to bring their catch
Home to the lair, as he did. It is myself I mean
And this girl, Electra. We stand here in your sight

258 **my sister's cruel sacrifice** Iphigeneia, sacrificed by Agamemnon to win the gods' favor at the outset of the Trojan War

Two children, fatherless, and both alike
Cast from our homes. Our father
Was lavish in his tithes to honor you.
Destroy his young, you will look hard to find
Another hand so generous to feast you.
If you suffer the eagle's progeny to die
Who will believe you when you manifest yourself
Hereafter? If this ministering branch   280
Is left to wither, when the day comes round
To serve the altar, it will not be there
To wait on you with sacrifice. Take heed:
You may uplift this house and make it great
Although it seems to lie in ruins now.

   CHORUS. Children, saviors of your father's house
Be silent, or some tattletale will warn
Our overlords. I hope I live to see them
Dead, and burning in the spitting fire!

   OR. One thing will never fail, the potent oracle   290
Of Apollo. It was he who bade me walk
This perilled way, and in the secret hours
Whispered to me a litany of horrors
To turn my blood to ice, should I neglect
To hound my father's murderers and kill them
As they killed him, round on them, gore them,
Strip them of all they have. If I should fail,
He said my own self would be forfeit; I should suffer
Miseries uncounted . . . he made it plain
And told how, when the dead are angry,   300
Their rancor rises as a pestilence
Up through the ground, to ride upon our bodies,
Creeping, feeding; cancer sets its teeth
In flesh once fair, and leaves its mark upon

---

291 **Apollo** god of prophecy and Orestes' patron; see note on
v. 31

Our faces, scabbed with silver scales.
He spoke of other visitations too,
Of Furies forming in the father's blood.
Dead things work by dark. Then murdered men
Come crying to their kin "Revenge!" and terror stalks
310 By night, to haunt him. Wild hallucinations
Come vivid on his eyes, although he screw them
Tight shut in the dark, and drive him forth
With barbs and scourges from the land that bred him.
For such an outcast there can be
No common bowl, no loving-cup,
No prayer at altars—there a sentry stands,
His father's ghost; no man will share a roof with him
Or take him in, till friendless and unmourned
He shrivels up and dies in misery.
320 Such was the oracle. Could I then deny it?
Even if I could, the deed must still be done,
For there are many calls on me, unanimous
To urge me on—the gods' commandment,
Grief for my father—there is weight in this—
The press of poverty, and my desire
That the marvel of the earth, my countrymen,
Whose glorious spirit subjugated Troy
Should not bow down before this pair of women—
For he is woman at heart; if I am one
330 He soon shall learn!

[ORESTES, ELECTRA *and the* CHORUS *join in a lament
over the tomb*]

  CHORUS. O you presiding Destinies
By the will of god make ending
In the turnabout of justice.
Let hate cry quittance to hate once spoken.

So Justice proclaims herself aloud, exacting
Atonement; blood for blood
And stroke for stroke, do and be done by;
Thus the lesson three ages old.

OR. O terrible my father,
What word of mine, what act   340
Can blow fair to the far shore,
Where fast you lie, a light
The measure of your darkness?
And yet it has been called
A work of grace, to tell old glories
In mourning for the champions
Of the house of Atreus fallen.

CHORUS. Child, when a man dies flesh is frayed
And broken in the fire, but not his will.
He shows his wrath though late.   350
For the dead man there is mourning,
For the guilty man a finding,
And the deathsong for a parent and a father
Is a call to judgement, ranging through
The universe disquieted
To hunt and find.

EL. Hear me in turn, my father,
My weeping and long sorrow.
Here two children at your graveside
Raise our chant for the departed.   360
Your tomb is haven
For outcasts, and for those

347 **Atreus** Agamemnon's father

Who pray for aid. What here is good,
What refuge from calamity?
Can we try a fall with fate?

CHORUS. Even from such as these the god
At will can shape a gladder strain,
And from the lamentation at the graveside
A song of triumph may arise
370 Within the palace, to carry home
The well-beloved, the dear unknown.

OR. If you had only died, my father,
At Troy, upon the field of honor,
And struck down by a foreign hand.
Then had you left your house
A legacy of glory, to your children
As they walked abroad, undying
Regard; then had you made
A heavy tomb upon a foreign shore
380 But for your family light burden.

CHORUS. Welcome then would he have gone
To those who loved him, to the nobled dead,
And in the nether world
Would have kept high state, in honor
Held and majesty, first minister
To the most mighty, to the kings of darkness.
For he was monarch on earth, and ruled
Those who command men's lives, who wield
The sceptre of dominion.

390   EL. No, that was not a place
For you to die, my father,
Under the battlements of Troy,

And by Scamander's ford to find
A plot of ground among the herd,
The reaping of the spear. Far better
That those who killed him should have died as he did,
And in far countries strangers to our sorrow
Had heard tell of the manner of their passing.

CHORUS. Child, you talk of riches passing mortal,
Of miracles, felicity   400
They only know who live beyond the wind.
Dreams are free. But the double scourge
Beats louder in the land; beneath
The earth there is a mustering
Of forces in our aid; our lords
Have hands unclean, and the curse is on them;
The children's day is coming.

OR. There now is a word
To rivet the ear. O Zeus,
Zeus, send up from below   410
The laggard punisher
For men of wrath and guilty hand
And let the score be settled for the parents.

CHORUS. May it be given me to raise
A cheer at the slaying of the man,
The woman's dying. Why should I hide
The thought that deep within flies free?
For in the voyage of the heart
There is a freight of hatred, and the wind
Of wrath blows shrill.   420

393 **Scamander** river of Troy   401 **who live beyond the wind**
the legendary Hyperboreans, who lived in the far north and
were particular favorites of Apollo

EL. Zeus two-fisted come
To smite them, yes, to smash
Heads; let there be a place
For faith again; where there is wrong
I say let right be done; O hear me
Earth, and dignities of darkness.

CHORUS. This is the law. Blood spilt upon the ground
Cries out for more; the act
Of desecration is a summons to the Fury
430 Who for the dead once fallen heaps
Havoc on havoc, new upon the old.

OR. O potentates of darkness, see,
See, curses that come mighty from the dead,
The house of Atreus, all that is left of us,
Helpless, driven from our rightful homes.
Where is there aid, O Zeus?

CHORUS. And my heart too has quivered
To hear your sorrow's utterance.
At such a word came despair,
440 A shadow on the heart. But when
I see you standing strong, there comes
Hope, and lightening of sorrow
At this fair sign.

EL. What shall our tale be then? What other
Than sorrows suffered for our parents' sake?
Fawn away, there can be no assuaging.
Anger ravens wolfish and implacable,
Child of the mother.

CHORUS. As in Aria the women beat their breasts
Then beat I mine, and in Cissian style   450
Made show of mourning. There was a sight
Of drumming fists, of blood-bruised flesh,
A dance of hands, plucking
Higher, lower, till my sorry head
Rang with their hammering.

EL. O ruthless, O relentless, O my mother,
Who in forced and meagre offices
Thought fit to bury him, a king
Far from his folk, without
The rites of mourning,   460
Without a tear, your husband.

OR. In such dishonor, say you?
But she shall pay for slighting him,
My father, by the help
Of the immortals, by the help
Of these my hands.
So let me kill her, and then die.

CHORUS. This too you must know. His limbs were
       lopped
And travestied, upon her word
Who ordered this his grave,   470
Intent to lay crushing grief
On your young life.
So was your father slighted.

449 **Aria, Cissian style** regions in Asia Minor. The chorus liken
their reaction to Agamemnon's death to that of professional
Asiatic mourners, with the difference that their grief was sincere.

EL. As you tell it, so he died. I was not by;
I had no rights there, I was nothing,
Only a cur that must be locked away
Inside, for fear she'd bite. I hid
The welling of my grief
Though tears came readier than smiles that day.
480 Hear this, and write it in your memory!

CHORUS. Yes, write, and let the tale bore deep
Into your heart. But bide your time
In patience still. So stands
The story now. You yearn
To know the end. Steadfast
Comes fittest to the fight.

OR. Pay heed, my father. Work beside your own.
EL. Your weeping daughter adds her voice to his.
CHORUS. And so cries all this company together.
490 Obey, and come to light; make one
Against your enemies.

OR. Battle now match battle, right with right.
EL. O gods, bring justice and accomplishment.
CHORUS. Fear comes over me as I hear you pray.
Long destiny has waited; now
When summoned it may come.

O curse inborn, sour song
Of fate, the bloody chastisement.
O hard and heavy sorrows, grief
500 That has no easy end.

The cure is in the house, not brought
By other hands from distant places

But by its own, in agony and blood.
Thus we sing unto the dark ones.

  But listen to our prayer, O blessed ones
Below, and send your willing aid
To these the children. Let them fight and conquer.

  Or. Father, who died out of the royal way,
I pray you make me master in your house.
  El. I ask a like gift from your hands, my father: 510
Aegisthus' death, a husband for my own. . . .
  Or. So when there is feasting here on earth
May you come welcome. If not, in the banquet days
When steaming meats are offered to the dead
No portion shall be yours.
  El.   Let me but come
Into my own, and on my bridal day
I'll bring gifts from the mansions of my fathers
To pour for you, and honor this tomb above all others.
  Or. Earth, loose my father. Let him see my fight.
  El. Queen Persephone, give us grace and strength. 520
  Or. Remember your laving and your death, my fa-
     ther—
  El. Remember the strange weaving that you wore—
  Or. Hobbled in fetters forged by no man's hand, my
     father—
  El. And wrapped about in shroud of foul devising—
  Or. Do these taunts sting you from your sleep, my
     father?

520 **Persephone** wife of the god Hades and Queen of the
Underworld   521 **your laving . . . strange weaving** Clytemnestra murdered Agamemnon in his bath, having entangled him
in his own robe. It is this robe that Orestes displays to the
chorus later in the play, vv. 1058ff.

EL. And do you lift the head that we so love?

OR. Send forth your chastisement to fight with those
You love, or let us turn the hold on them
If you would change defeat to victory.

530   EL. And father, hear this cry, my last:
See these nestlings huddled on your tomb
And pity them, the girlchild and the boy together.

OR. And do not write an end to Pelops' line.
Through them you live, though you are in your grave.

EL. For when a man has died, his children keep
His fame alive; we are the corks upon the net
That hold the skein from sinking in the waters.

OR. For you these tears, so give them heed.
Reward our speech, and save yourself.

540   CHORUS. The tomb lacks nothing of its honor now.
Long have you spoken, and the debt of tears
Is paid. But if your mind is firm to act
Go on, and make experiment of fate!

OR. So be it. But there is a question still to ask
And to the point. Why did she send
These offerings? What persuaded her to make
These late amends for sorrow long past healing?
A miserable favor, lavished on
The dead, the mindless! What these gifts might mean
550 I could not start to guess. How small they weigh
Beside her sin! Spend blood, there needs no more,
And you may spend the world to pay for it
And lose your labor. Thus the proverb runs.
Speak, if you know. You'll find a ready ear.

CHORUS. I saw, and know, child. There was a dream,
A horror in the night; she woke in fear

---

533 **Pelops** remote ancestor of the house of Atreus

And sent these offerings in mock of piety.

   Or. What did she dream? If you know, tell all.

   Chorus. She gave birth to a snake—this was her story.

   Or. And then? What was the sequel to this tale?   560

   Chorus. She wrapped it like a babe in cradle clothes.

   Or. What did it ask for food, this beast new-born?

   Chorus. In the dream, she gave it her own breast to suck.

   Or. How could she, and the nipple not be torn

By this foul thing?

   Chorus.   It sucked milk and clotted blood.

   Or. No riddle here. This vision means a man—

   Chorus. Then she awoke, and screamed in terror,

And in the dark house at the mistress' cry

The shuttered lamps began to blink their eyes;

And thinking to find surgery for pain   570

She sent at once these offerings to the dead.

   Or. I pray this earth, my father's sepulchre,

That this dream find accomplishment in me.

Thus I interpret; it is of a piece:

The serpent came from that same place

That brought forth me; she wrapped it in the robes

That cradled me; its mouth spread on the breast

That suckled me, and with lifegiving milk

Drew clotted blood, and at this dreadful thing

My mother screamed in fear; then surely she   580

Is doomed to die, and by no gentle hand

For bringing such a fearful prodigy

Into the world, and I am made the snake

To kill her, as this dream foretells.

   Chorus. Then you are the interpreter I trust

And cry amen. Expound the rest

To your friends now, who is to work, who wait—
   Or. It can be quickly told. My sister must go home
   And see that nothing of our plan leaks out,
590 So they who killed by treachery a man
   Deserving of great honor, may be caught
   By treachery, and in the selfsame net
   May die; for thus Apollo prophesied,
   The prophet-god who never yet has lied.
   Accoutred like a traveller I'll come
   Before the outer gates, with this man here
   Whose name is Pylades, my friend, the bounden
   Champion of me and mine. We'll both
   Assume the accent of Parnassus, and talk
600 The way men do in Phocis. If nobody
   Opens the gates for us and bids us welcome
   Because the house is busy with its troubles,
   We'll stay where we are, so anyone who passes
   Will point and say "Is Aegisthus home?
   Does he know they are here? Then why
   Does he bar his doors to those who ask shelter?"
   And if I gain admission at the gates
   And find that man upon my father's throne
   Or if he comes to look me up and down
610 And question me to my face, before he says
   "Where is this stranger from?" I'll strike him dead,
   And in the flashing of a sword he'll fall.
   So the Fury, that has never yet been starved of
      slaughter,
   Will drink pure blood, the third draught and the last.

---

600 **Phocis** district on the northern shore of the Gulf of Corinth,
containing Mount **Parnassus**, traditional home of the Muses,
and Delphi, the shrine of Apollo

[*To* Electra]

Your part to manage everything within
The house, so all may hang together,

[*To the* Chorus]

And yours, to keep a guard upon your tongue,
Speak when you should, be silent when you must.
And all the rest I summon this one here
To oversee, when I have made   620
All ready for the trial at arms.

[*Exeunt* Orestes *and* Pylades *to disguise themselves,*
      Electra *to the palace*]

  Chorus. Great the progeny of nature, strange
And dreadful; in the cradle of the sea
Lurk monsters; in the hinterland
Of earth and heaven, fire
Has wings to fly; and birds
And creeping things can tell
The malice of the stormwinds.

  But who could put to words the vaunting
Pride of man, the overmastering   630
Selfwill of woman, bedfellow
Of sorrows for mankind?
For when her passion turns
From wedlock and home, no beast
Or man can rage as she.

  Let him who has a mind to plumb the depths

619 **this one here** without the stage gesture which would
originally have accompanied these words, it is impossible to
say who is meant. It could be Pylades, Agamemnon or Apollo.

Of things, learn how the sad Althaea once,
Armed with prescience of fire,
Devised death for her son, and burnt
640 The red brand that was of an age with him
Since he came forth crying from his mother's womb,
Whose span was his, to the appointed day.

   There is another written black in story,
Scylla, who dealt in death, and was seduced
By enemies to kill one of her nearest.
Tempted her bitch-heart was and won
By Minos' gift, the necklace wrought of gold,
To cut from Nisus as he heedless slept
The lock of lasting life; and from this world went he.

650   And now I have begun this bloody history
Should there not be a place
For the loveless wedlock that this house
Would fain see gone? You came
In guise of enemy upon
Your husband, working on him with
Your wiles, and sly as only woman may,
On your husband armored strong in might,

637 the chorus offer examples from mythology of women who
have been carried away by their passions. **Althaea** was the
mother of Meleager. When her son was born the Fates told her
that he would die when a brand then burning in the fire was
consumed. She promptly extinguished the brand and locked it
away. When Meleager grew to manhood, he quarrelled with
his mother's brothers and killed them. In her grief and anger
Althaea rekindled the brand and Meleager died. 644 **Scylla**
daughter of **Nisus**, king of Megara, often confused with the sea
monster of the same name. Her father's life depended on a lock
of red hair growing on his head. **Minos,** King of Crete, who was
attacking Megara, persuaded Scylla to sever it, thus killing Nisus
and causing the surrender of the city.

And over him you prized
A house whose hearth is barren of its fire,
The heart of the man-woman.   660

  Of all the evils that the world can tell
Lemnos takes pride of place, a name
To fright the ear, a blasphemy,
And whatsoever dreadful thing
Shall pass, there will be one to christen it
"The crime of Lemnos." So angry were the gods
That from earth the race has gone dishonored.
For what is evil in heaven's sight
Is so for men. Does any of these tales
Not fit our case?   670

  Now stands the sword at the lifebreath
To thrust sharp home, and at the hilt
Is Justice aiding; for it is not fit
That those who trod the majesty of Zeus
Underfoot, should not be trampled
Down in their turn.

  Now the anvil of Justice stands foursquare
And Fate the swordsmith has the edge made keen.
For from the abyss of her mind the Fury,
Late come to honor, visits on the house   680
The child of blood shed in the former time
To make atonement.

[The palace. ORESTES *and* PYLADES, *disguised as travellers, come to the door and knock]*

662 **Lemnos** island off the coast of Asia Minor whose women,
according to tradition, had risen against their husbands and
killed them

OR. Boy, do you hear? There's someone knocking!
Is anyone there? Boy, I say! Who's at home?
For the third time, somebody come to the door,
If there is still shelter to be had here
Now that Aegisthus is in charge.

PORTER [*Within*]. All right, I hear you! Where are
you from?

OR. Go tell the masters of this house.
690 They are the ones I seek. I bring strange news.
And hurry; night's dark chariot comes
Apace; this is the hour
When merchants must drop anchor in a house
That opens up its doors to travelling men.
Send us someone in authority,
The mistress, or her man, for preference.
With women we must be polite, and talk
Around the matter. Man to man speaks straight
And to the point, without prevarication.

[*The door opens. Enter* CLYTEMNESTRA]

CLYTEMNESTRA. Travellers, you have only to state
700 your needs.
Such entertainment as this house can offer
Is at your command—a warm bath, or a bed
To magic weariness away, and honest
Eyes to wait on you. But if
You have more weighty business to discuss,
That is the man's work, and we shall inform him so.

OR. Daulis is my home. I am a traveller from Phocis.
I was on my way with merchandise to Argos
On business of my own. When I turned off here,
710 A man I had met—we were strangers to each other—
Asked my destination, and told me his.

He was Strophius the Phocian—that came out
In conversation—and he said to me
"Since you must go to Argos anyway,
Think to look out the parents of Orestes
And tell them he is dead. Do not forget.
Whatever his family decides to do,
Whether to bring him back, or have him buried
Out of his land, to lie forever among strangers,
Bring word accordingly, when you come back again, 720
For we have done but this—shed proper tears
Above his ashes, and unfolded them
In the belly of a brazen urn." That was all he told me.
But whether I talk to those who have
Authority and interest in this business
I do not know. I think his father should be told.

    CLYT. Oh,
You tell of how the waters of our grief
Rise clear above our heads. O curse upon our house
That ever throws disaster in our way,
How little slips your eyes, with what sure aim   730
You send your shafts to strike down from afar
Even the things that carefully were set
Out of your path, to strip me desolate
Of those I love. So now it is Orestes,
He who was so well schooled to tread around
This slough of death. There was a hope
Of decency, of revel in our house;
By this we kept alive; now take that hope
And by its name write "Liar."

    OR. I would have rather introduced myself   740
To entertainment so munificent

712 **Strophius** friend to Argos, to whose hands the infant
Orestes had been entrusted

By telling of more pleasant things; for none
Could be more anxious to oblige than travellers
Their hosts. But I should have looked upon myself
As breaking a sacred trust, if I neglected
To carry this matter through. I gave my promise
To Strophius, and am under obligation
To you now, as your guest.

    CLYT. This changes nothing. You will be received
750 According to your merits, and shall have
No less regard, while you are in our house.
If it had not been you who brought this message
It would have been another. It is now
The hour when footsore travellers should reap
The promise of their long day's march.

[To her servants]

Take him inside, to the guestrooms where
We lodge the menfolk, his attendants too
And fellow travellers. See that they receive
The comforts proper to a house like ours.
760 You have your orders. You are answerable to me.
I shall go tell the master of the house
What I have heard, and with my friends about me
Take the measure of this new disaster.

[CLYTEMNESTRA, ORESTES *and* PYLADES *go inside the
palace*]

    CHORUS. Come friends and fellow servants all,
Is it not time for us to show
The power of our voices, and so aid
Orestes? O sovereign Earth and sovereign
Mound of the tomb, who lie upon
The body of the sealord and our king,
770 Now hear us, grant us aid.

Now is the time ripe for Persuasion
To marshal all her wiles
And for the god of the dark journey, Hermes,
And him that dwells in night, to stand
Sentinel as the sword comes to the match.

[*Enter* CILISSA]

The harm must be afoot, the traveller is busy—
Here is Orestes' nurse in tears.
Where are you going from the gates, Cilissa,
With misery, the uninvited guest
Free ever of her company, to step beside you?   780
    CILISSA. Our mistress sent me hurrying to find
Aegisthus for the travellers, so he
Could talk to them man to man, and learn
The ins and outs of what they have to tell him.
She had a wry face for her servants, but behind
Her eyes she hid a smile that things had worked
So well for her—but for this house
It's nothing short of tragedy—the tale
The travellers told, and that's plain enough.
And it will be good news to that one   790
When he hears it. Oh, the pity of it!
All the troubles that we had, and never
Two alike, here in the house of Atreus,
More than a body could stand; oh, how they vexed
This heart of mine! And yet I never
Had to endure anything like this.
The rest I got through when I set my mind to it.
Orestes, bless him, plagued the life out of me—
I had the rearing of him from his mother,
And all those times he got me up   800

774 him that dwells in night Agamemnon

By crying in the night—and what good did it ever
Do me? Babes are little animals,
They can't think for themselves, you have
To guess what they want, what else can you do?
The child in his cradle doesn't have the words
To tell us if he's hungry, if he's thirsty,
Or wants to wet; no arguing
With young insides. I needed second sight,
And I was often wrong, believe me, and had to be
810 His washerwoman too. Feed him, clean up after him,
It was all the same job, and I
Doubled these offices, ever since I took
Orestes from his father's hands; and now
He's dead, they say; so much the worse for me.
Well, I must go to find the man who ruined
This house, and he'll be glad enough to hear it.
    CHORUS. Did she say he was to come in state?
    CIL. Say that again, so I may catch your meaning.
    CHORUS. With his bodyguard, or by himself?
820   CIL. She told him to bring his servants armed—
    CHORUS. Then as you hate your master, do not tell
      him this.
Say he must come alone, so his informants
May talk without constraint. Bid him hurry
And be of good heart. It is the messenger
Who takes the crooked word and makes it straight.
    CIL. But are you happy over what I told you?
    CHORUS. And if Zeus means to send a wind
To blow away foul weather?
    CIL.   How?
Orestes is dead; the house has lost its hope.
830   CHORUS. Not yet. He would be a poor diviner
Who traced things so.
    CIL.   What do you mean?

Do you know something we have not been told?

    CHORUS. Go with your message, do as you are bid.
The gods will take care of their own affairs.

    CIL. I'll go, and do as you have told me;
And heaven grant it turn out for the best!

[*Exit*]

    CHORUS. Grant this my prayer, O Zeus
The godhead, father of Olympus,
That those who long to see
This mansion set to rights may have their hope   840
Accomplished; what I have said
Is nothing if not just, O Zeus;
Do you enforce it.

    O Zeus, rank him who now
Is in the house above his enemies.
For if you raise him to eminence
Two and threefold will he repay you,
Zeus, and cheerfully.

    For be advised, this colt,
The orphan of a man much loved,   850
Is harnessed in the chariot
Of suffering; and you must set a measure
To the course, so we may never
See him break step, but extend himself
Full tilt across the ground.

    O Zeus, rank him who now
Is in the house above his enemies.
For if you raise him to eminence
Two and threefold will he repay you,
Zeus, and cheerfully.   860

And you that haunt the inner sanctum of the house
In pride of wealth, O gods
That think as we do, hear us.
Come, rid us of this bloody stain
Of things done in olden time.
Make manifest your justice, let
Old murder breed in the house no more.

And you who live
At the mouthpiece of the world
870 Grant to those who fell in glory
This kindness, that they may look up again
To the house of a hero, and that eyes of love
May see it as a beacon shining, free
From enshrouding shadows.

And let the son of Maia give us fitting aid
For he is mightiest
To give a deed fair passage
If so he will, for many a time
He deigns to make the dark word plain
880 Or wraps the eyes in shadows, speaking
Riddles that no clearer come by daylight.

And you who live
At the mouthpiece of the world
Grant to those who fell in glory
This kindness, that they may look up again
To the house of a hero, and that eyes of love
May see it as a beacon shining, free
From enshrouding shadows.

869 **the mouthpiece of the world** the meaning of this whole
passage is obscure; probably Apollo's shrine at Delphi is meant
875 **the Son of Maia** Hermes

Then at last will the house be rid
Of double evil; with united voice   890
We shall speed the work, as women may,
Break out the mourning song, and sing
"The ship sails fair."
Mine, mine to reap the argosy, and wreck
Is far from my beloved.

When the time comes for doing, be
Stoutedhearted; when she calls
"My child," shout her down
With cry of "Father," and act
The sin that is grace, her murder.   900

And with Orestes' mind combine
The heart of Perseus; for your friends
On earth and under it, perform
This favor, though it sting you sore.
Let death and blood
Run wild within, and bring upon the man
Who killed, a death in punishment.

[*Enter* AEGISTHUS]

AEGISTHUS. I do but as they bid me, and am come
In answer to the message. There are people
Lodging here, they say, who tell a tale   910
We never hoped to hear, the death
Of Orestes. This house has wounds still raw
From bloodshed long ago; now must it take
Another burden on itself, a thing
Of running blood? What can I make of this?
The living truth? The terrified imaginings

902 **Perseus** mythical hero who killed the Gorgon, she-monster
with hair of snakes whose glance turned men to stone

Of women make bubble-tales that burst
Upon the air. Can you say anything
Of this, to make me certain in my mind?

 CHORUS. We heard the same. But go in to the travel-
920 lers
And let them tell you. It is better always
To go to the source than learn secondhand.

 AEG. Yes, I should like to see this messenger
And ask if he was with him when he died
Or speaks the words of groping rumor only.
The mind must have an eye for trickery.

[Exit]

 CHORUS. Zeus, Zeus, what shall I say? And where be-
gin
My prayer for the gods' aid?
How, before the ending, find
930 Words worthy of my will?
For now the bloody cutting-edge
Comes close, to rend a man.
Now in the house of Agamemnon
Will he bring ruin upon all
Or light the fire of liberty again
And in the kingdom of his father
Live rich, the honored son.
To such a wrestle must Orestes come
The challenger, by the gods' advisement
940 One against two; and may he throw them!

[A cry within]

Ah, what is that?
What has happened in the house?
Let us stand aside till the work is finished
So there may come no blame on us all

In this foul business, for the fight
Is at an end.

[*Enter* SERVANT *from the palace*]

SERVANT. Cry desolation, for our lord is dead,
And cry again, a triple cry of sorrow!
Aegisthus is gone. Come, no delay;
Open the portals of the women's chambers,   950
Slide back the bolts; we need young strength
To fight for us, a man, but not for him
Who is dead and gone; no purpose there.
Ahoy, ahoy!
I call on the deaf, on those who lie
In idle slumber and do nothing. Where
Is Clytemnestra, what does she do now?
Her head is on the block, and soon
Must fall, in measure as she did to others.

[*Enter* CLYTEMNESTRA]

CLYT. What is this? What means this shouting in the
    house?   960
SERVANT. Listen to me. The dead are killing the liv-
    ing.
CLYT. You speak in riddles, but I read you well.
By sleight we killed, by sleight we are to die.
Come, hurry, bring an axe to kill a man.

[*Exit* SERVANT]

Let us make certain, then. It must be he or I,
So far have I come now in this sad history.

[*Enter* ORESTES *with a drawn sword,* PYLADES *beside
    him*]

OR. You are the one I seek. His part is played.

CLYT. Are you dead, my love? Is brave Aegisthus
  gone?
OR. You love that man? Then in one tomb you shall
970 Be buried, and be faithful after death.
CLYT. Hold back, my son, have pity on this breast
My child, where often slumbering
You lay, and suckled milk to make you strong.
OR. Pylades, what shall I do? How may I kill my
  mother?
PYLADES. What of the oracles still unfulfilled
Apollo spoke at Delphi? Your sworn promise?
Better the world should hate you than the gods.
OR. Your word has won. You show the way that I
  must go.

[*To* CLYTEMNESTRA]

Come in, for I would kill you on his body.
980 In life you thought him better than my father;
Then sleep with him in death, if such you love
And give to him whom you should love your hate.
CLYT. You took my youth. May I not share your age?
OR. You killed my father. Would you share my
  house?
CLYT. The blame is Destiny's as well as mine.
OR. Then it is Destiny who kills you now.
CLYT. Have you no terror of a mother's curse?
OR. You bore me and then cast me out to sorrow.
CLYT. To live with friends. This was no casting out.
990 OR. I was born of a free father and you sold me.
CLYT. Then where is the price that I received for
  you?
OR. I could not bring myself to tell your shame.
CLYT. Tell all, but tell your father's follies too.
OR. Blame not him. He toiled, you sat at home.

CLYT. Women suffer when the man is gone, my
   child.
OR. Man's labor feeds the women who sit idle.
CLYT. My child, I think you mean to kill your
   mother.
OR. I will not kill you. You will kill yourself.
CLYT. Take care. Your mother's curse will hound you
   down.
OR. My father's curse will find me if I fail.   1000
CLYT. This is the serpent that I bore and fed.
OR. Indeed the terror of your dreams spoke true.
You sinned in killing. Now be sinned against.

[ORESTES *and* PYLADES *drive* CLYTEMNESTRA *into the*
                     house]

CHORUS. Even for these I can find tears, and for
Their coupled death. But since Orestes has been bold
To top this long and bloody history
We find it better that the light within
The house not be extinguished utterly.

   In time there came to the sons of Priam
Justice heavy in punishment   1010
And on the house of Agamemnon came
The lions paired to battle two.
Then pressed he to the uttermost, the exile
To whom god had spoken, eager
Under heaven's admonition.

   Cry joy now for the mansions of our lords,
The end of pain, the end of rich things wasted
By two in infamy, the dark days gone.

   He came; and his part was to deceive,

1020 To scheme and conquer. In the fight
His hand was guided by the very child
Of Zeus—we mortals know her name
As Justice, and we have good cause—
She who in a blast of hate
Comes on her foes destroying.

Cry joy now for the mansions of our lords,
The end of pain, the end of rich things wasted
By two in infamy, the dark days gone.

As Apollo spoke from his deep-riven
1030 Cavern on Parnassus, so
Has it passed; the innocent deceit
Comes home to fight harm grown old.
Divinity has ways to keep
From going down to evil; it is fit
That we should laud the powers that reign in heaven.

Now is there light to see, the bit
Is gone that held our house so hard.
So up, you halls, arise; for time
Too long have you lain fallen.

1940   Not long, and Time that brings all
To pass will enter in
Our gates, when the evil presence
Is cast from our hearth, and ceremonies
Have made all clean; then chance
Will come up ever fair for those
Who take their lodging here in aftertime.

Now is there light to see, the bit
Is gone that held our house so hard.

So up, you halls, arise; for time
Too long have you lain fallen.   1050

[*The doors open.* ORESTES *is seen standing sword in
hand over the bodies of* CLYTEMNESTRA *and* AEGISTHUS.
He holds the robe in which AGAMEMNON *was killed*]

OR. See here the double lordship of this land
Who killed my father and laid waste my house.
A while they sat upon their thrones in state,
And they are lovers still, as you may judge
By what befell; their oath has kept its promise.
Together they swore to kill my wretched father
And die together; they are not forsworn.

[*Displaying* AGAMEMNON's *robe*]

See too, all you who look on this sad story,
The trick they used to bind my wretched father,
Chains for his hands, a halter for his feet.   1060
Come, spread it out and make a circle round
To show this net to catch a man.
So may the father see—I mean not mine,
But he who watches every living thing,
The Sun—my mother's filthy handiwork.
So at the judgement day, whenever it shall come,
He may appear to testify
That I had just cause to pursue the death
Of this my mother. On Aegisthus' death
I waste no words. It is written, adulterers   1070
Shall be punished—but she who worked so vile a thing
Against her man, whose children she conceived
And bore beneath her cincture, sweet load once,
Now this you see, a curse, a thing of hate—
What do you think her now? A water-snake, a viper
Who needs no fangs, whose very touch

Will rot a man, so venomous
Her mind, so quick to strike . . .
And this, what shall I call it? Has it any name
1080 That one may say with decency? A snare
To catch an animal, a winding sheet,
A tenting for the bath? A net, a skein
We well could say, a robe to hobble feet—
The sort of thing a cozener might use
Who lived by catching travellers and robbing them
Of money; such a trick as this
Would win him many victims, and would keep
His heart warm inside him. . . .
May such a woman never come to share
1090 My home and bed; may heaven first destroy me,
Before I have begotten me a child.

    CHORUS. Sing sorrow for things done:
For you a hateful death, and for the one
Who lives, the ripening of pain.

      OR. Did she do this or not? This mantle testifies
That it was dyed red by Aegisthus' sword.
Dip it and dip again, and still
The stain of blood and its accomplice, Time,
Have spoilt the work. Now I can praise him, now
1100 Make lamentation over him; and when
I speak to this, the robe that killed my father,
I sorrow for the doing and the death,
For all our race, the tainted prize
Of this, my inconsiderable conquest.

      CHORUS. No mortal man can live his life
Through to the end untouched by suffering.
There is trouble here, and more to come.

      OR. But hear me now; I cannot see the end;
My chariot has run me from the course,
1110 My rebel senses lead me where they will,

While fear draws breath to sing within my heart
And it must dance to his angry tune. While I
Have wits about me still, I call upon my friends
To hear. I killed my mother, but I say
There was some right in this; my father's blood
Had tainted her, she was a thing unclean
In heaven's sight.
And for the blandishments that made me bold
To such a deed, I cite as culpable
Apollo, seer of Delphi, who proclaimed in oracles   1120
That I could do this thing and still
Be innocent; but if I failed—
What then would come on me I will not say.
Draw bow at hazard, you would never
Come within measure of my suffering.

[*He arrays himself as a suppliant*]

See me how I go forth, with wreath
Upon my head, with branch in hand,
To the centrestone of earth, Apollo's seat
And holy shrine, that famous place
Whose fire burns everlasting; I will go   1130
Out from my own, from blood that is my own;
Apollo charged me that I should not turn
To any other sanctuary but his.
To all who live in Argos in the future time
I say remember how these evil things were done
And speak for me when Menelaus comes.
And I shall go an outcast from my land
To walk among strangers, and leave behind
In life, in death, this memory of me.

1126 **wreath, branch** customary emblems of the suppliant
1136 **Menelaus** Agamemnon's brother

CHORUS. What you did was well. Do not let foul
1140 speech
Harness your mouth, or turn your tongue to evil.
For you brought liberty to all who live
In Argos, when you came upon
This pair of snakes and cut their heads off clean.

[ORESTES *points and cries out*]

OR. O servants of this house, they come
In shapes of Gorgons, clad in robes of black,
Their hair a nest of snakes; I cannot stay!
CHORUS. If any man has earned a father's love
You are the one; so what imaginings
1150 Are these, that send you reeling? Stay,
Be bold, you have good cause.
OR. I suffer, these are no imaginings
But real; the hounding of my mother's hate.
CHORUS. It is the blood still wet on your hands
That comes on you now to shake your senses.
OR. O Lord Apollo, are they coming yet?
They weep, their eyes are running foul with blood.
CHORUS. There is one way to purify yourself. Apollo
Will lay his hands on you, and make you free
1160 Of this affliction.
OR. You do not see them, but I see them.
I must go forth, I can stay here no longer.

[*Exit*]

1146 **Gorgons** Orestes sees the Furies advancing on him, still
invisible to the chorus. They were traditionally represented as
women with hair of snakes and carrying blazing torches—thus
resembling the Gorgons, to whom Orestes compares them. See
note on v. 902

CHORUS. Good luck go with you, then, and may the
   god
Look kindly on you, and preserve you safe
In fortune.
Now for the third time
Has storm come from the race, to blow
Upon the palace of our kings, and passed.
One was the child-feast,
The grief and desolation of Thyestes.   1170
Two was the death of kings, when the lord
Of the Achaean host was struck
Down in the bath.
Three was the coming of the savior
Or death—which shall I call it?
When will there be an ending, when
Will wrath be spent, and fate lulled to slumber?   1177

1169 the child-feast Atreus, Agamemnon's father, had killed his
brother Thyestes' children and served them up as a feast
1172 Achaean Greek

THE EUMENIDES

DRAMATIS PERSONAE

THE PYTHIA, priestess of APOLLO
APOLLO, God of Prophecy
ORESTES, son and murderer of CLYTEMNESTRA
HERMES, messenger of the gods
GHOST of CLYTEMNESTRA
CHORUS, of FURIES
ATHENA, patron goddess of Athens
WOMEN of ATHENS, attendants of ATHENA

Herald and jurymen of the Court of Athens

SCENE: first, before APOLLO's oracular shrine at Delphi; later, Athens.

THE EUMENIDES

[*Before* APOLLO's *shrine at Delphi. The* PYTHIA, *his
priestess, stands in solitary prayer*]

PYTHIA. First in my prayer I honor Earth
Who first of gods gave oracles to men,
And then to Themis, who second came
To hold this seat of prophecy, her mother's,
As legend tells; and in the third succession
By Themis' free consent, with violence to none,
Another earthchild, Titan-born,
Came to inhabit it, and this was Phoebe,
Who gave it as a birthgift to Apollo.

Eumenides like *The Libation Bearers*, the play is named for
its chorus, otherwise called Erinyes or Furies. The title Eumenides, literally "the kindly ones," is often applied to these
beings, either by confusion with other more beneficent underworld powers, or euphemistically, in the hope that they would
respond kindly to being addressed by such a name. Here the
title could have specific reference to the Furies' change of
nature at the end of the play.

Pythia an old woman, inspired prophetess of **Apollo,** whose title
comes from the monstrous Python, serpent killed by the god on
his first visit to Delphi

1 First in my prayer the Pythia traces the history of the Delphic
Oracle from the earliest supernatural powers. **Earth,** offspring
of Chaos, was regarded as a vaguely personal goddess; **Themis,**
her kin, later came to be the embodiment of righteousness;
Phoebe, daughter of **Earth,** belonged to the race of **Titans,** the
giants who were earth's first inhabitants; in one account she
is mother of Leto (see v. 379) who is mother of Apollo

10 So from her name he takes his name of Phoebus.
   He left the quarried waterland of Delos,
   Put in at Athens and her harbored shore,
   And so came here, to live upon Parnassus.
   The sons of Hephaestus built him roads to send him
   With honor on his way, and made
   His rough path straight; the people of this land
   And Delphos, then their lord and governor,
   Lauded his coming. Zeus invested him
   With prophecy, and set him on the throne
20 As oracle, the fourth to hold this office.
   So is he prophet for his father Zeus.
   These are the gods to whom I speak my prelude;
   And in my invocation she that lodges
   In the forecourt of our shrine, Athena, has high place;
   And with her I must rank the nymphs in honor,
   Who have their home in Corycus, the cave
   Where birds find welcome, and the spirits walk.
   And Bacchus too—for I am not unmindful—
   Has made his home among us, from the time
30 When he came godly with his legion of mad women
   To harry Pentheus like a hare to death.
   I call the stream of Pleistus, and Poseidon
   In his majesty, and Zeus all-powerful, almighty,
   And go to sit upon my throne and prophesy.

11 **Delos** island in the Aegean, birthplace of Apollo   13 **Parnassus** mountain overlooking Delphi   14 **Hephaestus** god of craftsmen   17 **Delphos** here introduced as the origin of the name Delphi, though the word properly means "womb"— Delphi was regarded as the geographical center of the earth   28 **Bacchus** Dionysus, god of wine and revels, worshipped particularly by women in orgiastic ceremonies   31 **Pentheus** early king of Thebes, hostile to the worship of Dionysus. As punishment he was torn apart by the god's frenzied worshippers, among them Pentheus' own mother, who in their madness took him for a lion   32 **Poseidon** God of Oceans

May they look with favor on my going in
More now than ever in the former time.
If there are Greeks here, let them now draw lots
And enter, according to the custom; and I
Shall give them counsel as the god inspires me.

[*She enters the shrine. After a brief pause she reappears, terrified and barely able to stand*]

Things terrible to tell, things terrible   40
For eyes to look upon, have driven me
Out from Apollo's house again.
My strength deserted me; lock-limbed
I crawled away, could walk no more.
An old woman afraid is nothing, she is
A child again.
As I approached the sanctum garland-gay,
I saw upon the centrestone a man
Obscene in heaven's sight, who had come
To have his sins washed clean; his hands ran blood,   50
He held a new-drawn sword, a branch
Cut high upon an olive tree, and twined
With clustered wool, as the good custom is,
A blazoned fleecing—this I can say sure.
In front of him on the benches sat
A wondrous company of sleeping women—
And yet not women; Gorgons, I should say,
And yet no Gorgon ever looked like these.
There was a picture that once I knew
Of creatures bearing off the feast of Phineus—   60

48 **centrestone** the omphalos, conical stone within the shrine at
Delphi, believed to be the navel of the world. See v. 17   51
branch . . . fleecing traditional emblem of the suppliant   57
Gorgons fabulous monsters, women with hair of snakes   60
Phineus mythological character constantly plagued by winged
monsters who stole his food

But these have no wings, they are black
And horrible to look upon, they snore,
And where their breath has blown no man may pass.
Their eyes are foul and running, their apparel
Is not such as one should bring into the sight
Of holy images or halls of men.
I have never seen the tribe which owns
This company, nor what place on earth could boast
It farrowed them, and does not repent its labor.
70 What shall become of them I leave to him
Who is master here, Apollo; he
Is strong to heal and prophesy, and wise
In prodigies; for he has come
Into homes of others and made them clean.

[*Exit. The doors of the shrine open, revealing the centrestone.* ORESTES *sits upon it with* APOLLO *and* HER-
MES *standing beside him. On the ground at his feet are
the huddled bodies of the sleeping* FURIES]

APOLLO. I shall not fail you. Whether I
Am near to you or far, I shall be beside you
Watching to the end, and those who seek
Your hurt shall find me no mean adversary.
And for the present you may see
80 The raveners are overmastered, these
She-abominations have succumbed to sleep,
These hoary children of old time, whose company
Is shunned by god, by man, by very beast,
Who were begotten on this world for evil, whose do-
        main
Is evil, sunless Tartarus below earth,

85 **Tartarus** one of several names for the kingdom of the dead

Whom earthlings and high gods look upon and shud-
  der.
But keep your pace and show no slackening;
For over land and longshore they will follow
Hunting, over every plodding mile,
Beyond the island cities of the sea.   90
And show no weariness; this bitter pasturage
Is yours, until at last you come
To Athena's city, and take sanctuary
Before her ancient image, grasping it;
And there, with judges appointed and with medicine
Of words, we'll find a way
To rid you of these pains forever; for
It was by my mandate that you killed your mother.
  ORESTES. O Lord Apollo, to you is known
The way to keep from evil. To this knowledge   100
Add care that these things do not slip your mind.
You have power for good. In this we trust.
  AP. Remember, then, and never
Lose heart from fear.
[*To* HERMES]   And you, blood of my blood,
Child of my father, Hermes, watch over him.
You are called the god who guides. Be true
To your name now, and guide my ward
To green fields. Such as he have rights
Divinely given, and upheld by Zeus.   110
Forth to the world he goes. Give him godspeed.

[*Exeunt* ORESTES *and* HERMES. APOLLO *retires inside
the shrine. The* GHOST *of* CLYTEMNESTRA *appears above
the sleeping* FURIES]

  CLYTEMNESTRA. What, sleeping? Shame! What use
    are you asleep?

Of all the dead must I alone
Want honor at your hands? Because of those I killed
I wear the brand of shame conspicuous
Among the dead; I am driven in disgrace.
I say to you that these hold me most guilty.
But I too suffered from my nearest kin,
And yet no power bestirs himself for me,
120 A mother murdered by her very child!
See these gashes, mark them in your heart.
In sleep the mind has eyes to see
Our destinies, though the eye of day is blind.
Your lips came greedy to the offerings I poured,
No wine, but drink more sinister to lull you,
And solemn feasts I set for you by dark,
Your witching time, upon the burning place.
And now I see you tread them underfoot.
The man has gone like a fawn slipped from the snare
130 And bounded free, though you on every side
Held nets to catch him; he has made you things of
    scorn.
Listen to me. It is of my life
That I have spoken here. Take thought, you goddesses
Of the underworld. I, the dream of Clytemnestra,
Call on you now.

(*The* FURIES *whimper*)

Well may you whine. The man is far away;
He has protectors, and they are not mine.

(*they whimper again*)

You sleep too long, my sorrows cannot move you.
Orestes, mother's murderer, is gone.

125 **more sinister . . . you** the murder of Agamemnon and
Cassandra

(*they growl*)

You growl, and still you sleep. Will you not rise?   140
What have you ever done but mischief?

(*they growl again*)

Sleep and long labor, arch-conspirators,
Have drawn the serpents' fangs.

(*they give two sharp howls*)

CHORUS. At him, at him, at him, at him. Watch out!
CLYT. You dream of hunting, belling like the hound
Whose mind is ever on the chase.
What are you doing? Up! Let not your labor
Leave you wanting, or caressing sleep
Make you forgetful of your hurt. There should be pain
Inside you, as of just reproach; for those   150
Who know their duty, this should be a whip to drive
      them.
Blow from your bloody mouths on him, belch
Hot smoke to stop him in his tracks;
Follow again, and this time shrivel him.

[*The* GHOST *disappears. The* FURIES *stir in their sleep
      and begin to rouse each other*]

CHORUS. Wake up, and wake her too, and I
Will waken you. What, sleeping? On your feet,
Shrug off this slumber, let us see
If there is fault in our first dealings.

[*Perceiving that* ORESTES *has gone*]

O sisters, we have suffered wrong.
Much have we undergone, and all in vain.   160
Here there is hurt for us, here sorrow,

Here intolerable pain; he has slipped
The net, our quarry, and has gone
His way; I was won with sleep
And let our prey pass by.

O son of Zeus, you have taken what is ours,
And in arrogance of youth come rampant
Over us, the grey ones; you succour
Your suppliant, this blasphemer, who showed
70 His parent small love—snatched away
This mother-slayer, you, a god!
In this where is there justice?

In my dreams came a taunt, a biting
Under the skin, to quicken my heart,
Like the racewhip that comes curling
Under bellies of linked horses.
Now I must flinch and again, tormented
Under the whiplash of the torturer.

Such are the actions of the younger gods
80 Who come usurping, who would rule all.
Now is a sight of the throne running blood,
At its head, at its feet; on the centrestone
Is defilement, the grim
Mark of a man's blood, curse and horror.

So has the prophet-god defiled
His own home, fouled his secret place
At no man's bidding, and by invitation
Of none but himself. He holds
Men in honor, sets rule of gods aside
90 And turns the ancient Destinies to nothing.

166 son of Zeus Apollo

So has he won my hate, and still will never
Set his man free. Though he fly
Beneath the earth, there shall be no escape
For him; he shall go guilty,
And there will be a new avenger
Come upon his head to punish him.

[APOLLO *reappears from the shrine*]

AP. Out! I command you leave this house
At once; it is the home of prophecy,
No place for you—unless you would feel
The bite of a snake, a silver snake   200
Sped from a golden string, and in agony
Spit out the black and bubbling blood
You have sucked from men, clotted vomit
Of former victims that you fed upon.
This house is no fit place for such as you.
Yours is the bloody judgement seat, where heads
Roll, where there is gouging out of eyes,
Spoiling of fatherhood and boys' young glory gone,
Where men are crushed under stones and lose
Their precious parts, where there is groaning   210
Of malefactors spitted upon pikes. Do you hear
What I say? Such is the banquet where
You long to be. For this you are detested
By the immortals, and your outward looks
Show what you are. Such things as you
Should live in caves where lions rend their prey,
Not bring your foul contagious company
Into this place of divination. Go
Upon your goatish and unherded way; no god
Would joy in pasturage of such a flock.   220

200 **a silver snake** his arrow

CHORUS. Now you must listen, Lord Apollo, in your
  turn.
You have no little guilt in this.
All is your doing, all the blame is yours.
   AP. How? You may speak so far, to answer me.
   CHORUS. It was your oracle that told
The wanderer to kill his mother.
   AP. It was my oracle commanded him
To avenge his father. So?
   CHORUS. And then you took it on yourself
230 To have him here, with blood fresh on him!
   AP. Yes, it was by my order
He came here, to have his guilt washed clean.
   CHORUS. Then you blame us, who brought him on
  his way!
   AP. Because you are not fit to enter here.
   CHORUS. This is the duty that is laid upon us.
   AP. What is your office, then? What post of honor?
Speak it aloud.
   CHORUS.   When men have killed
Their mothers, we must drive them from their homes.
   AP. And if it is the wife who kills her man?
240   CHORUS. The blood that she sheds is not her own.
   AP. Are you so scornful? Do you count as nothing
The pledge that Zeus gave Hera, when he took
The goddess to wife? According to your argument
The Queen of Love, the fountainhead
Of man's most dear delights, must have no honor!
The love of man and wife is warranted
By divine law, it is greater surety
Than sworn oaths. If they are to kill each other
And keep your favor, if there is to come from you

244 **Queen of Love** the goddess Aphrodite

No punishment, not so much as an angry glance,   250
I say you have no right to pursue Orestes—
For you come down stern enough on him, I see,
And in the other matter show yourselves indifferent.
Athena in her divinity shall consider
The rights and wrongs of this.

> CHORUS. I shall never let that man escape.

> AP. Pursue him, then, and give yourselves more
>   labor.

> CHORUS. I have my privilege, and you shall never

Abridge it by your arguments.

> AP. I would not take such privilege from you.   260

> CHORUS. No, you need nothing. You are called great
>   already

In the shadow of Zeus' throne. But I,
Led by a mother's blood, will visit
Justice upon this man, and hound him down.

> AP. And I shall give the suppliant my strength

And protection; for there is terrible
Anger on earth and in heaven over such
A one as he, if I should wantonly
Fail in the help for which he has petitioned me.

[*The* CHORUS *goes off in pursuit of* ORESTES. APOLLO
*withdraws into the shrine. The scene changes to Ath-
ens.* ORESTES *is discovered kneeling as commanded
before the statue of* ATHENA]

> OR. Lady Athena, I have come   270

By order of Apollo; greet this wanderer
With favor. I am not here to seek
Riddance of guilt, my hands
Are not unclean. The raw edge of my sin
Is blunted, rubbed away among the traveled
Paths of men, in other homes and places.

And when I went by land, or when by water,
I always kept Apollo's oracle
Inviolate. Now to your dwelling-place
280 And image have I come, O goddess; here
I keep my vigil, and await the end,
The trial that is to be.

[*Enter the* Chorus *of* Furies]

Chorus. Here are the tracks of the man-thing clear,
Mute witness; follow where they point the way,
Like hounds baying after a wounded fawn.
As the blood drops we will hunt him down.
Hard have we run and long, breast heaving
Murderous; the whole world wide
Have we herded him, and over seas
290 Wingless we came pursuing from the sky,
Pacing his scudding ship. And now
He is somewhere hereabouts and hiding;
The smell of blood comes greeting me.

[*They urge each other on*]

Cast about, cast about;
Hunt everywhere, for he
Must not slip us again, the matricide
Must pay his price.

[*Seeing* Orestes]

He is here, he has found
Strength, he has twined arms
300 Around the image of the deathless goddess
And would from her claim settlement.

But that may not be. A mother's blood
Once shed on the ground is no light thing

To recover; quick it runs
On the earth and is gone.

[*To* ORESTES]

But you must give me blood
In turn to drink, blood rich red
From your warm lithe body;
So could I fix on you drinking
Sustenance, the draught of sorrow.   310
   And I shall suck you dry untimely
And drag you down to make
Requital for the death-throes of your mother.

And whosoever among men
Has sinned against god, whoever
Has to his friend or dear parent
Been forsworn, there will you find them,
Receiving each his merited reward.

For there below ground
Sits the Dark God, strong   320
To call men to judgment; he sees
All, and writes it in his memory.

OR. I have been seasoned in adversity, and know
The riddances of evil, when to speak
And when be silent. In the present case
I have advisement from a wise instructor
To give tongue, for the bloodmark now
Is spent and fading from my hand.
The stain of matricide is washed away,
For in the mansion of Apollo, at   330

320 **Dark God Hades,** God of Death

The god's hearth, while it was fresh upon me still,
I sacrificed a pig to purge myself.
It would be weary work to catalogue
The many I have visited who took
No harm from my converse. Time grows old,
And all things with it; so their danger dies.
Now with lips pure and unsullied I invoke
The mistress of this land, the goddess
Of Athens, to come to my aid; so may she win,
340 Without a blow struck, me and all my people,
The land of Argos, in sworn alliance
Of everlasting friendship. Whether she
Is in the land of Libya, by the flowing
Waters of Triton that for her
Were birthright, where with mantled feet
Or barefoot striding she administers
Aid to her friends; or whether manly
And imperious she keeps bold watch
Over Phlegra's plains—gods have long ears—
350 I pray her come, and bring to me deliverance.

    CHORUS. Apollo shall not save you, nor the redoubt-
      able
Athena. None shall mark your passing,
And in your heart you will have found no joy,
But be a bloodless thing, picked clean
By the dark spirits, hollow. Will you answer me
No word? Will one who has been bred for me
And to me consecrated, show so insolent?

---

344 Triton . . . birthright Athena's birth had some mystical
connection with water, according to some accounts with the
stream cited here. But the tradition is very obscure, and the
main function of this reference and that to **Phlegra** which fol-
lows is to illustrate the vast extent of Athena's domain   349
Phlegra mythical site of battle between gods and giants, vari-
ously identified

You shall not die on the altar; I shall feed
Upon you as you live. Now listen
And we shall sing our binding song.   360

   Come, let us link and dance,
For it is our intent to set
Our terror to a tune, and tell
How this our company apportions
The governance of man.
This we believe; we stand for straightforward
Justice. If a man can show clean hands
Our wrath is not visited upon him, he
Can pass his days untroubled.
But if there be any like this man   370
Who has sinned, who has bloody hands to hide,
Then we come, stern incorruptible
Spokesmen of the dead, last arbiters
To exact his own life's blood.

   Night, O my mother, from whose womb
I took my being, your child,
The scourge of those that have eyes to see
And those that walk in darkness, hear me!
For Leto's cub would disentitle me
And rob me of this cowering prey   380
Who is mine alone, by right of law
And shedding of a mother's blood.

   And so, over the sacrifice,
This my song to make men mad,
To hammer wits, scatter senses wild,
No mortal music, but the binding song

379 **Leto's cub** Apollo. **Leto** was a mortal woman beloved **of**
Zeus

Of the Erinyes, taking
The reason captive, coming dire
On ears of men.

390   Such is the office Destiny
Inexorable has spun for us
To have and to hold for ever:
If a man should wanton walk
With crime, wherever he should go
We go, till he passes down
To the underworld, and he shall find
In death no great deliverance.

    And so, over the sacrifice,
This my song to make men mad,
400 To hammer wits, scatter senses wild,
No mortal music, but the binding song
Of the Erinyes, taking
The reason captive, coming dire
On ears of men.

Such is our birthright. It is not for any
Of the deathless ones to touch it, or demand
A part in what is given as my portion,
Nor in their white vestments have I right or claim.

    I have elected overturn
410 Of houses. When the battlespirit
Shows within doors, and levels
Near and dear, we come pursuing
The offender, and though he be strong
We grind him down, by token
Of the blood fresh on him.

We are earnest here. These concerns belong
To us and no other. If the gods
Have any part in our decisions
It is to stand aside and ask no questions,
For Zeus cares not to see the blood upon us   420
And has declared us outcast and detestable.

I have elected overturn
Of houses. When the battlespirit
Shows within doors, and levels
Near and dear, we come pursuing
The offender, and though he be strong
We grind him down, by token
Of the blood fresh on him.

Lustre of man walking proud beneath the sky
Diminishes to nothing and goes unregarded   430
Down, when our black-mantled company
Has passed, and danced antic over man's dominion.

Sheer from the sky I come,
A giant pouncing, drop deadweight
Upon him, grind him underfoot,
And he trips and falls, the long race run
And lost; for him there is no easy ending.

He falls, and does not know that he is falling,
For he is mad, the sickness of guilt
Dark overclouds him, and plaintive rumor   440
Tells of a mansion fallen among darkness.

So it stands. We are quick in the finding
And sure in the ending. We possess

A memory for evil, and we stand
Aloof, impervious to prayers of men.
We do the work that is apportioned us
Without esteem or honor from the gods
And sundered from them in a light
That never shone by day. And this the path,
450 The rugged way that all must go,
The seeing and the blind together.

Then is there any among mortal men
Who is not humbled and afraid, to hear
The power that heaven has allotted me
By law, and ratified by Destiny?
So I am endowed for perpetuity;
This my privilege endorsed by time,
Nor, though I have a place appointed me
Below earth, where I must live forever
460 Barred from the light of sun, must I
Ever behold my authority diminished.

[Enter ATHENA *in her chariot]*

ATHENA. I heard from afar off your call for aid,
Over by Scamander, as I staked my claim
In the land the Greeks, their kings and their command-
ers,
Made over in my name, great part
Of their rich winning, to be mine forever
Root and branch, a gift of special favor
To the sons of Theseus. So I came
Untiring on my way, and harnessed
470 Speeding steeds to this my chariot.
And when I see what company has come

463 **Scamander** river of Troy   468 **Theseus** legendary King of
early Athens

Now to our land, there is astonishment
At such a sight, no fear. What sort of thing
Are you? It is to all of you I speak
These words—to this man couching at my image
And seeking me to sponsor him, or you,
Who look like nothing sprung from seed, like nothing
That ever gods' eyes looked upon, and yet
Not like the forms of men. Yet this
Is a place of righteousness, and it forbids   480
Even the innocent to speak ill of his neighbour.

CHORUS. Daughter of Zeus, your questions shall be
    answered
In short measure. We are the ageless daughters
Of night, and in the underworld
That is our home we are called Curses.

ATH. I know your provenance then, and a name to
    call you.

CHORUS. It will not be long before you know our of-
    fice.

ATH. Speak to be understood, and I might know it.

CHORUS. We hunt from their houses those that kill—

ATH. How long? What ending have you set the
    killer?   490

CHORUS. A place where joy is a word without mean-
    ing.

ATH. Is it for this you come in full cry after him?

CHORUS. He thought it good to murder his own
    mother.

ATH. Was there not another charge he feared to of-
    fend?

CHORUS. What spur so sharp, to make him kill his
    mother?

ATH. There are two sides here. We must still hear
    the other.

CHORUS. Put him on oath! There is nothing he could
  say!

ATH. Oaths are not everything. Right must be done.

CHORUS. Question him. Let us have straightforward
  justice.

500 ATH. Are you willing to entrust this case to me?

CHORUS. What else? You were born to be obeyed.

ATH. [*To* ORESTES] Well, friend? What answer
  would you make to this?

But tell me first your country and your birth
And something of your history; and then
Defend yourself against these accusations,
Given that you come here armed in right
To keep your vigil at my image, as
Ixion did before, and are entitled
To a fair hearing. These are my questions.

510 It is your turn now. Give me plain answers.

OR. Lady Athena, let me make
Your ending my beginning, and remove
This weighty reservation. It was not
In search of absolution that I came,
And when I took my seat beside your image
My hands were guiltfree. I shall give
Proof positive of this. A man
With blood fresh on him is debarred by law
From speaking, till a suckling animal

520 Is sacrificed, and he has been anointed
With its blood by one in whom power is invested
To purify. I was made clean long ago
And in another house, by running water
And offering of beasts. So I dismiss
This scruple. Let me now in brief

---

508 Ixion the Cain of Greek mythology, the first to murder one
of his kin, and purified of his offence by Zeus

Recount my lineage. I was born in Argos,
And my father . . . you may well ask of my father. . . .
His name was Agamemnon, lord of ships,
And he was your companion, when you made
A desolation where a city stood   530
In Troy. So he came home and died,
Nor was there any honor in his passing;
For in the blackness of her heart my mother
Killed him, secretive and devious
With nets to bind; and these remain, to tell
His laving and his slaughter. I,
Who was an exile in the former time,
Came to my home again, and killed
My mother, I will not deny it,
And took a life for life, in vengeance   540
For my beloved father. If I am
Accountable in this, Apollo too
Must answer for it; for he goaded me
With threat of pain and torment if I failed
To visit retribution on the guilty.
Whether I was right or wrong in this
Is for you to judge. No matter what
Becomes of me, I shall accept your verdict.

   ATH. This is great matter, more than any mortal man
Can think to judge; and even I have not the right   550
To sit in judgement on a murder done
On the spur of anger, all the more since you come law-
    fully
To throw yourself on my protection, and you bring
No damage or defilement on my house.
You come with clean hands, and I judge you fit to stay
Here in this city. But these too have their office
Which cannot be neglected. If they fail
To carry off the victory in this,

In future time they may direct their barbed malevo-
    lence
560 Into our soil, a pestilence downpouring
To poison it for ever. So the issue stands.
We have a choice. He stays here, or
He goes; and either way must mean
Heartsearching and much sorrow.
But since the judgement of this case has fallen
On Athens, I shall delegate a court
To sit upon this murder under oath, and give it
Jurisdiction for all time to come.
And you must call your proof and testimony
570 To give your arguments sworn warranty. I shall return
When I have made election of my citizens,
Which is most fit to serve, and to decide the case
Impartially. They shall be sworn to keep
An open mind, and judge it on its merits.

[*Exeunt* ATHENA *and* ORESTES]

CHORUS. Now will the new dispensations
Bring havoc, if the plea and detriment
Of matricide prevail; far and wide
Will men look upon these dealings, and be
Seduced to approbation. So
580 Over and again in the future time
Will children test the mettle of their valor
In working violence upon a parent.

Then we shall come, our coven, not withholding
Anger till a man has shown himself
In works, but slaughtering haphazard.
The word will fly lip to lip, and men
Will read engraven on their neighbours' faces
The wrath to come; although they seek

Surcease or remedy, feeble ever
Will be the uses of consolation.   590

And when the blow has fallen
Let no man call vociferous
On Justice, or the Erinyes throned
In majesty. So might you hear
A father crying, or a mother lately
Come to sorrow; but the edifice of Justice
Is fallen out of its old dignity.

In the scheme of things there is a place
For fear; in men's hearts it should hold
Tribunal, watching; and it profits us   600
To come to wisdom under the duress
Of suffering. If man or his city
Have never walked in fear, where should they ever
Learn to bow down humble before Justice?

The life ungoverned and the life too strait
Avoid, for though the works of god
Are devious, it is the middle way
He prizes. And I will utter
A maxim of like measure: insolence
Is very child of vanity.   610
But out of healthfulness of heart
Comes happiness, the loved and sought.

And in all your doings keep this in heart:
Humble yourself before the shrine of Justice
And never in contempt of holy ordinance
Spurn it underfoot, with view to profit;
For punishment will follow certain sure
At the end. Thereto let every man

Honor his father and his mother, and
620 The guest that lodges within his gates.

    And he who walks willing and unforced
In paths of right, shall be no stranger
To joy, nor will he ever be
Utterly confounded. Yet I say
The man who wanders from the narrow way
And stops at nothing to amass his wealth
Sooner or later, if he will or no,
Sees his mast fall stricken down, and he
Must strike his sail discomfited.

630   Then in his agony he calls
Lone in the tiderace, and none answers.
And there is laughter in heaven at the man
Who cried "Such could never come to me"
Distraught and powerless to rise
Above the waters. After long
Continuance of prosperity
He strikes the reef of Justice, and goes down
Unwept into oblivion.

[*Enter, in procession,* ATHENA, ORESTES *and a jury of
Athenian citizens. They take their places to form the
court, with* ATHENA *presiding*]

    ATH. Herald, make proclamation, call the host to or-
    der.
640 Let man give to the Etruscan clarion
Its complement of breath, and send its call
Incisive into the assembly.

640 Etruscan clarion shrill trumpet

For as they take their places on the seats
Of counsel, we may use this silent time
To tell my citizens in convocation
Of the ordinance I have established for eternity,
And these too, so their case may have fair trial.

[*Enter* APOLLO]

CHORUS. Apollo, rule your own domain. What inter-
    est
Have you in this case? Answer me.
    AP. I am here on two counts—as a witness, for Ores-
        tes   650
Came to my hearth and home a suppliant,
And it was I who cleansed him of the blood
Upon him, as in duty bound—and then
As his advocate; it was on my account
He killed his mother.

[*To* ATHENA]

Proceed, then. I shall leave it to your wisdom
To see that all is done in proper form.
    ATH. [*To the* FURIES] You have our ear. I declare
        the court in session.
The prosecution may commence, and set
The facts in proper order.   660
    CHORUS. We are many, but our argument is brief.

[*To* ORESTES]

Answer my questions as I ask them. First,
Did you kill your mother? Yes or no?
    OR. Yes. Of this there can be no denial.
    CHORUS. The first round is ours, and two to follow!
    OR. Do not brag before your enemy is down.

CHORUS. How did you kill her? Tell me that.

OR. I tell you. With my naked sword I slit her throat.

CHORUS. Who was it counselled and persuaded you?

670 OR. His oracles: the god who is my witness.

CHORUS. The Prophet counselled you to kill your mother?

OR. He did, and so far I have no complaint.

CHORUS. You will say otherwise if they convict you.

OR. I have no fear. My father sends help from the grave.

CHORUS. Trust in the dead, when you have killed your mother!

OR. She was disgraced, she was twice culpable.

CHORUS. How so? Explain your meaning to the court.

OR. She killed her husband, and she killed my father.

CHORUS. But death has cleared her. You are living still.

680 OR. Why did you not hunt her while she was alive?

CHORUS. The one she killed was none of her own blood.

OR. Am I of one blood with my mother then?

CHORUS. Yes, murderer; for how else did she make you
In her womb? Do you disclaim your mother's blood,
Your own life's blood—

OR.   Apollo, testify
For me, and show if I was just to kill her,
For facts are facts, I cannot deny them.
But was this bloodshed justified or not
In your mind? Answer one way or the other,
690 So I shall know how to reply to them.

AP. Gentlemen of this high court of Athens,

My plea is a just one. I am the Prophet,
And cannot lie. From my prophetic seat
I never spoke one word of man, of woman, of cities,
That Zeus my father did not order me.
There is justice here. I bid you mark
How strong it is, and let my father's will
Dictate your actions, for there is no oath
That can outrank the dignity of Zeus.

    CHORUS. Zeus, you say, gave you this oracle   700
To tell Orestes, that when he had taken
A life to pay his father's, he should make
No retribution for his mother's life?

    AP. The cases are not equal. Here died a noble man
Gifted by heaven with majesty and honor,
And by a woman's hands—no Amazon
Who drew her bow on him and shot him down
In honest fight, but as I shall explain
To you, Athena, and to these appointed
By lot to sit in judgement on this case.   710
He came home from the wars. He had come off
With credit, all considered, as men of good will
Admitted. She lay in wait for him.
He bathed himself, and when he neared the ending
She caught him in a mantle; no escape
For him, she fettered him in cunning folds
And cut him down.
Now you have heard it. Thus died a man
Above all others estimable, lord of ships.
As for the woman, I have shown her   720
For what she was, and with intent to grieve
The people's hearts, for they have been appointed
To arbitrate in this.

706 Amazon legendary race of warrior women

CHORUS. Then Zeus, according to your argument,
Holds it of more weight when the father dies.
But it was he that bound his aged father Cronus!
How do you reconcile your argument with this?

[*To the jury*]

Gentlemen, I recommend this to your notice!
   AP. Animals! Blasphemous abominations!
730 What he has tied he can untie again;
There is remedy for this, a thousand ways
To give release; but when a man
Is dead, when the dust has drunk his blood,
There is no raising him, no magic word
My father has provided for this case.
On all things else he has but to command
Or countermand, whichever way he pleases;
He need but nod his head and it is done.
   CHORUS. Suppose you win. Suppose he is acquitted.
740 Look what must follow. He has spilt
His mother's blood upon the earth,
Blood that was his. Shall he then
Go back again to Argos, to inhabit
The house that was his father's? Will he find
Welcome where men kneel in prayer together,
A brotherhood to give him membership
And holy water?
   AP. I will tell you. Listen, you will see that I am
     right.
Although the child is said to be the mother's,
750 She is not the parent, only the custodian
Of the new seed. He that mounts her is the parent.
She keeps the seed—she is no part of it

726 **Cronus** father of Zeus, overthrown by him as he had
overthrown his own father

Or it of her—until it grows, god willing.
I shall give you proof of my arguments. A father
Does not need a mother to make children. There is one
At hand to prove this, daughter of Olympian Zeus.
She did not grow in dark within the womb
Yet no god could beget an offshoot fair as she.
In all things else, Athena, as best I know,
I shall make great your city and its host,   760
And I have sent this man as suppliant to your house
So that he might be yours for evermore,
And you, divinity, might win to your allegiance
Him and those after him in time to come,
A constant reassurance for posterity.

   ATH. [*To the* FURIES] Have you said your say? May
     I command
The judges to give their votes as they think fit?

   CHORUS. Our shafts are all shot, and it remains
Only to hear how the decision falls.

   ATH. So be it. [*To* APOLLO] What is it your pleasure
     that I do?   770

   AP. [*To the jury*]You have heard what you have
     heard. Now give
Your votes, my friends. Be mindful of your oath.

   ATH. People of Athens, the time has come
For you to hear my edict—you, the first
That ever sat in judgement over bloodshed.
This shall be the place where for all time to come
The people of Athens shall convene their court,
The hill of Ares, where the Amazons encamped
When they came invading in despite of Theseus.
They founded here and built their citadel   780
Whose ramparts rivalled his, and sacrificed

756 **daughter . . . womb** Athena had no mother, but sprang
full-grown from the head of her father Zeus 778 **Ares** God of War

To Ares. From his name this rock was called
The hill of Ares. Here Respect shall have its seat
Among my citizens, and by her side
Fear of Wrongdoing, own sister to Respect.
Day and night shall they preside among us,
Provided only that my citizens are willing
To keep their laws pure, and admit no influence
Defiling. When you foul clear water
790 With mire, you will have no drop left to drink.
Neither the life ungoverned nor the life too strait:
This is the rule I would have my citizens
Preserve and cherish—nor to cast out fear
Entirely from your city; for whatever man
Was righteous, if he knew no fear?
If you walk reverent in the world, right-fearing,
Then you will have a tower of strength to guard
Your city and your land, whose like
The eye of man has never looked upon,
800 No, not in Scythia, not in Pelops' country.
And this the council I establish here,
Compassionate and incorruptible,
Yet swift to anger, ever vigilant
Though others sleep, to ward our land from harm.
This, then, my lengthy exhortation to my people
For time to come. Now to the task in hand.
Let each man take his ballot and pass judgement.
Be mindful of your oath. My speech is done.

800 **Scythia** in what is now Russia, east of the Caspian Sea
Pelops' country the Peloponnesus, now the Morea, the large
peninsula of south Greece   801 **the council . . . here** Aeschylus here links his story with historical fact, suggesting a divine
origin for the Council of the Areopagus (literally, Hill of Ares,)
oldest Council of Athens   807 **take his ballot . . . judgement**
there are two urns, one standing for condemnation and one for
acquittal, into which the jurymen drop their votes as they think
fit

[*The jurymen file past the voting urns, dropping in their ballots*]

CHORUS. [TO APOLLO] We are dangerous company
for your land to keep.
I warn you, do not belittle us.   810
AP. And I tell you, fear the oracles spoken
By me, by Zeus, and do not make them void.
CHORUS. You harbor murder where you have no
right.
From this time forth your oracles are blemished.
AP. And had my father lost his wisdom, when
He harbored the first murderer, Ixion?
CHORUS. Say what you like. If judgement goes
against me,
I shall come heavy on this land again.
AP. The new gods and the old gods too
Hold you contemptible. The victory shall be mine.   820
CHORUS. So did you act in Pheres' house, persuading
The Fates to release a mortal from death.
AP. Is it not just, then, to repay fair treatment
With favor, all the more when the friend has asked it?
CHORUS. You made them drunk, those ancient god-
desses,
And took powers that were theirs by long right.
AP. This suit will not end in your favor. You
Shall vomit your venom, no opponent shall be hurt.
CHORUS. Since in your youth you override our age
I shall await the issue of this suit, and then   830
Shall know if I am angry with this city.

---

816 **Ixion** see v. 508   821 **Pheres' house** Apollo had, for an
offence against Zeus, been condemned to spend some time as
a serf in the palace of Admetus, son of Pheres. Admetus treated
him kindly, and Apollo rewarded him by making the Fates
drunk to avert his destined death

ATH. It is my task to give the final judgement here.
I shall award the ballot to Orestes;
For mother had I none to bring me forth.
Except in case of wedlock, my allegiance goes
Wholehearted to the male. I am my father's child,
And so I shall not count the woman's death
Of greater moment than the man she slew,
The rightful lord and master of her house.
840 So even with half the votes Orestes wins.
Now, jurymen who have been so appointed,
Empty the urns with speed, and let us see the votes.
    OR. Phoebus Apollo, how will it be decided?
    CHORUS. Night my dark mother, see what they do!
    OR. Here is my ending; the noose or the light.
    CHORUS. And mine; to grow in honor, or lose all.
    ATH. [*To the jurymen*] Shake out the ballots, friends,
      and number them,
And let there be no fault in the division.
Dire are the consequences of misjudgement,
850 And by one vote a house may stand again.

            [*The votes are counted*]

This man stands acquitted of the charge of murder.
The votes have fallen equally on either side.
    OR. Athena, you are savior of my house.
I was denied my fatherland, and you
Have given me a home again. In Greece
It will be said of me "This man once more
Belongs to Argos, and has come into
His sire's estate"—all thanks be to this trinity,
Athena, and Apollo, and the Savior
860 Who brings all things to pass—who looked
With pity on my father's death, who saw
My mother's advocates, and succoured me.

Now I turn homeward. To this land and host
I leave this pledge in perpetuity:
Never will governor of Argos come
With warlike preparation to this land;
For if any are unmindful of the oath I swear,
We who shall then be buried in our graves
Shall frustrate them, and bring all their works to noth-
    ing,
Confound their marches, and cast the evil eye   870
Upon their going, so they count the work ill spent.
But if there is uprightness, and they show
Continual honor to Athena's city
By union of arms, then we shall never
Cease from looking favorably upon them.
And so farewell. May you and all your people
Outmatch and overthrow all those who come against
    you,
To keep you safe, and crown your spears with glory.

[*Exit*]

CHORUS. Gods of the younger breed, you have ridden
Over the laws of ages, torn them from my hands,   880
And I am desolate, stripped of honor.
But I will come heavy in anger on
This land; then sorrow will match sorrow
When from my heart the black pus drips
Into your soil, and resource is there none.
Then will the land be blighted, there will be
Death of growing things and death of young ones.
Then for Justice! It will spread malign
Over earth's face, festering and mortal.
Shall I weep, then? For what will become of me?   890
Oh, I have borne what should not be borne
At this city's hands. O Daughters of Night,

Great is your grief, and little honor!
   ATH. Be advised by me, and do not take these things
Too sorely to heart, for you are not defeated.
The votes were equal and the sentence just.
It was not to spite you; there was testimony
Vivid from Zeus, and he who sent the oracle
Attested that no harm should befall Orestes
900 For doing what he did. So do not bow our land
   Beneath your anger, harbor no resentment,
   Nor bring us barrenness by witching down
   Such dewfall on us, to come ravenous
   And eat our tender seeds. I promise you
   By all that is holy, you shall have a place
   Among us, deep in consecrated ground,
   Where by rich altars you shall sit enthroned,
   By these my citizens enshrined and honored.
     CHORUS. Gods of the younger breed, you have ridden
910 Over the laws of ages, torn them from my hands,
   And I am desolate, stripped of honor.
   But I will come heavy in anger on
   This land; then sorrow will match sorrow
   When from my heart the black pus drips
   Into your soil, and resource is there none.
   Then will the land be blighted, there will be
   Death of growing things and death of young ones.
   Then for Justice! It will spread malign
   Over earth's face, festering and mortal.
920 Shall I weep, then? For what will become of me?
   Oh, I have borne what should not be borne
   At this city's hands. O Daughters of Night,
   Great is your grief, and little honor!
     ATH. No, you are not dishonored. You are goddesses,
   And should not on the crest of your anger obliterate
   A land of mortal men. By Zeus I stand;

And need I say that I alone of gods
Know the keys of his mansion, where his thunderbolt
Lies closeted? But there is no call for that.
Let me rather teach you reason: never spill   930
Your curses on this land, to blight
All that bears fruit. Let bitterness
And anger be stillborn. Live here with me
And share my prayers and honors. There is room
For both of us. And when my people for all time
Offer you first-fruits in hope of child
Or happy marriage, you will say that I was right.

    Chorus. That I should come to this—
The wisdom of ages, banished
Underground, contemptible!   940
Wrathful now my wind and wild.
What is this agony that comes
Insidious to my heart? O mother Night,
Be witness to my anger; I am made
The gods' fool, they have torn from me
My honor, turned the accomplishment
Of long time into nothing.

    Ath. I will bear with your anger. You are older than I
And by so much wiser; but to me Zeus gave
No mean intelligence. If you should go   950
Into the land of others, there will come a time
When you will look back longingly on Athens.
Take my word for that. Time in his courses
Will bring my citizens yet greater glory,
And you shall have your seat of honor by
Erechtheus' house, where such noble company
Of men and women shall wait on you as never
Was seen in any other land but ours.

956 **Erechtheus** fabulous king of Athens, supposedly born from
the earth

Nor must you ever scatter in my domain
960 Pricks of bloodhunger, out of which grows ugliness
In young men's hearts, a rage of drunkenness
That never came from wine, or put the hearts
Of cocks into the bodies of my citizens,
Factious to fight their own. If they want war,
Let them look wider; there are enemies enough
Lusting for glory. I do not reckon it
Combat, when fowls fight in their own yard.
Such the choice I can offer you. Do good
And be well done by; reap the honors due
970 To merit, and make yourselves a place
In the land loved by the gods above all others.

    CHORUS. That I should come to this—
The wisdom of ages, banished
Underground, contemptible!
Wrathful now my wind and wild.
What is this agony that comes
Insidious to my heart? O mother Night,
Be witness to my anger; I am made
The gods' fool, they have torn from me
980 My honor, turned the accomplishment
Of long time into nothing.

    ATH. I shall never tire of telling you the blessings
      that are yours,
So you can never say that you, a god
Of olden time, were cast out of our land
Without right or honor by me, a younger goddess,
And these my citizens. But if you grant
Due honor to Persuasion, who has come
To sanctify the sweet enchantment of my voice,
Then you might stay with us. But if you choose
990 Otherwise, then you may not justly turn your wrath
Upon our city, or afflict our men-at-arms

With your resentment. It is in your power
To have a just share in this land, and every honor.

CHORUS. Lady Athena, tell what place shall be mine.

ATH. One griefless and free from all pain. Accept it.

CHORUS. Suppose I do. What right remains to me?

ATH. This: no house flourishes unless you will it so.

CHORUS. You will do this, and give such power to
me?

ATH. And prosper every man who gives you honor.

CHORUS. Will you warrant me that these things shall
endure?   1000

ATH. I make no promises that I cannot fulfil.

CHORUS. You may win me, then; the anger is depart-
ing.

ATH. Take root here, and win friends to your side.

CHORUS. What blessings would you have me call on
Athens?

ATH. Such as belong to honorable victory—
From earth, and from the deep sea waters,
And from the skies above; winds to blow serene
Over our land; our tillage and our grazing beasts
To bring forth each according to his kind, and prosper
Our citizens unceasing; for   1010
The seed of man, safe deliverance.
And grant to those that live in love and faith
Longer succession. In this world as in a garden
The shoots I cherish are the ones that grow
Unblemished, that are sprung from upright stock.
Such it is in your power to grant. And when
War summons, and the cause is just,
I shall look to it that the world see us
Victorious, and award our city honor.

CHORUS. Where Athena stays, there too shall I
Receive a dwelling, nor shall ever   1020

Fail in allegiance to a city
Where Zeus reigns in majesty, and Ares,
This bastion of gods, for the land of Greece
A shining seat of worship, defender
Of the faith. With golden promise for the future
I call the splendor of the sun to draw
From the soil its benison, so you may be strong
And in life's fortunes ever prosperous.

1030   ATH. Such are my actions, ever provident
For these my citizens. I have won over
Great and jealous deities to dwell among you.
All of man's estate is given
Into their keeping
And he who never felt the weight of them
Shall be smitten in his life, and know not how or why;
For crimes inherited from past generations
Drag him before their judgement seat,
And cry he never so loud, Destruction

1040 Will never anwer him, but lay him low
In the bent of her anger.
    CHORUS. And I pray there may never come upon
Your trees a wind destroying—such
The blessing I pronounce—or sunburst
Out of time and season, blasting buds
Of grown things. May they never wither
Nor their fruitfulness fail. May Pan
Grant the flocks at the appointed time
Increase, making them bring forth twofold,

1050 And may the fruit of earth, the buried lode,
Be manifest, a rich endowment of the gods
And treasure for the finding.
    ATH. Wardens of Athens, do you hear these things

1047 **Pan** god of flocks

And what they portend? For the Erinyes'
Authority is great among the deathless gods
And those of the underworld. In the land of men
They come evident, to bring their purpose to fulfil-
    ment,
Teach some to sing, and to others' lives
Bring tears to make them blind.

  CHORUS. On Death I lay this interdiction,   1060
That it shall not fall untimely
On our menfolk. To grace of maidenhood
Grant good fortune and a life's partner,
You that have power; and grant it, O divine
Destinies, you sisters born
Of my mother; it is you who guide
Things aright, who in every home
Have footing, and time without end
Walk among men and level them with justice,
In all ways, of all gods most honored.   1070

  ATH. I am right glad for these sure promises
Of good intent towards my land,
And render thanks to Persuasion, who stood vigilant
Over my lips and speech, when these ones first
So savagely rebuffed us.
But Zeus was victor here, for he is god
Of councils; and my contentiousness
For good has triumphed over all.

  CHORUS. And I pray that faction, bellowing
And gluttonous of life and fortune, never   1080
Shall be heard within our city, nor
The dust drink of the black blood of our people
And angry thirst for more, afflicting us
With death in death's image, bringing down
A rage of destruction on our city.

But may they give each other comfort, living
In intent of common love, and hating
As with one mind; among the race of men
This for many ills is cure and answer.

1090   ATH. Are they taking thought to find the way
Of honorable speech?
From the terror writ upon their countenances
I see great benefit accruing for my people,
For if you will be kind as they are kind
And heap their honors, come what may
You will guide your land and city straight, and lead
        them
Into the paths of righteousness.

[*The* FURIES *prepare to depart for their new home*]

     CHORUS. Go with good fortune. Prosper and grow
        great.
Godspeed to the people of this city
1100 Whose seat is next to Zeus, who are knit
To the Virgin Goddess in bonds of love
And who at last have won to discretion,
Sheltered by Athena's wings, and ever
Rejoicing in the Father's sight.
     ATH. And to you godspeed. But I must go before
        you
To show your chamber by the sacramental light
Of these, your escort. And let solemn offerings
Go with you, as you make your way
Under earth. Keep imprisoned below ground
1110 Whatever may be harmful to our country,
And what may profit her, send forth
To give us victory.
And you who dwell in this city, children

Of Cranaus, go to guide them,
For they will live among you as your fellows,
And show them good intent that good may come.
   CHORUS. Farewell and once more farewell,
A double bidding, all of you who keep
Their habitation in Athena's citadel,
Both heavenly and mortal.   1120
Venerate my sojourn here, and use
Me kindly, and you will never
Chafe against the bitterness of life.
   ATH. To all your prayers amen. I shall conduct you
By radiance of torchlight to your dwelling place
Beneath the earth, to the dark underground,
And with us go these women, whose charge it is
To minister to my image. Flower of all the land
Of Theseus, let them come forth now, a noble com-
     pany
Of maids and matrons, and the elder women   1130
Banded together.
Vested in purple let them come resplendent
To do us honor. Let the torchlight go before,
So that the kindly company of these that share
Our land may show itself in strength of manhood
In time to come.

             [The procession forms]

   ESCORT. Go on your homeward way
In reverence exalted,
Children of Night grown old,
Jocund in processional.   1140

Let all around keep dignity of silence.

1114 **Cranaus** legendary king of Attica

To a dwelling old as time
In the earth's enfoldment,
In honors proud
And sacrifices and fair fortune.

Let all around keep dignity of silence.

   Visit our land, grave powers,
With grace and loving kindness.
Let fire feed on the torches
1150 And make glad your coming.

Now to our song make acclamation.

There shall be peace for ever
For Athena's people.
So has Destiny agreed
And Zeus all-provident.

1156 Now to our song make acclamation.

BIBLIOGRAPHY

THE ANCIENT THEATER

Arnott, P. D., *An Introduction to the Greek Theatre* (Bloomington, Indiana University Press, 1963).

Bieber, M., *The History of the Greek and Roman Theater,* second edition (Princeton, N.J., Princeton University Press, 1961).

AESCHYLUS AND GREEK TRAGEDY

Kitto, H. D. F., *Greek Tragedy* (New York, Doubleday & Co., Inc., 1954). *Form and Meaning in Drama* (New York, Barnes & Noble, Inc., 1960).

Murray, G. G., *Aeschylus, the Creator of Tragedy* (New York, Oxford University Press, 1940).

TEXTS

Aeschylus, *Agamemnon,* ed. J. D. Denniston and D. Page (New York, Oxford University Press, 1957).

Aeschylus, *Agamemnon,* ed. E. Fraenkel (New York, Oxford University Press, 1950).

The *Oresteia* of Aeschylus, ed. G. Thomson (New York, Cambridge University Press, 1938).

The above works contain the Greek text with plentiful notes and discussion. Thomson's edition also includes a verse translation; that by Fraenkel contains, in addition to an extremely detailed commentary on the *Agamemnon,* sections on *The Libation Bearers* and on the dramatic technique of the trilogy as a whole.